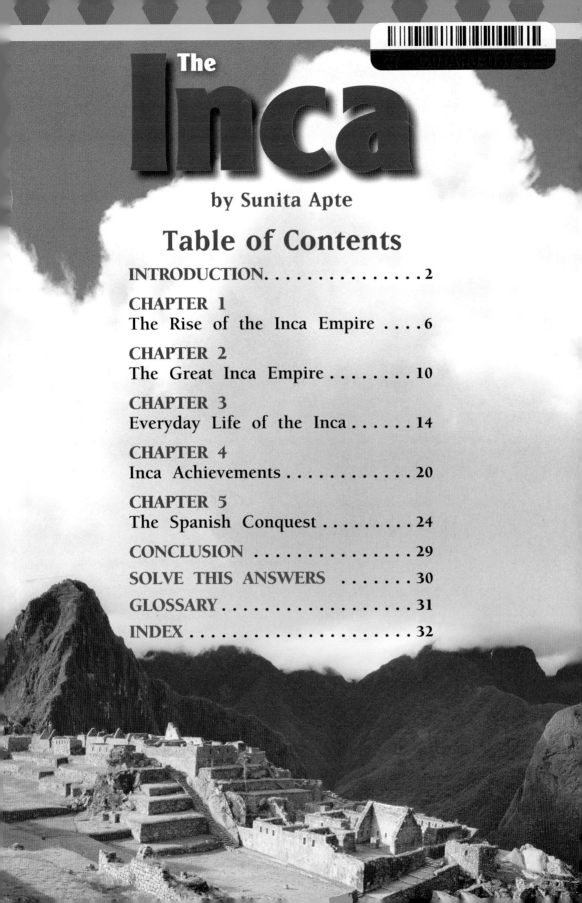

The Inca

by Sunita Apte

Table of Contents

INTRODUCTION

Imagine taking a trip to South America, to the city of Cuzco (KOOS-koh), Peru. Cuzco is high in the Andes (AN-deez) Mountains. If you walked the streets of Cuzco, you would see many things. You would see huge walls made of giant stones. You would see women wearing colorful skirts and hats. If you closed your eyes, perhaps you could picture the temples and gold statues that used to fill the streets.

The Andes Mountains are 4,500 miles long (7,200 kilometers). Many peaks are more than 20,000 feet (6,100 meters) high!

Cuzco was the capital city of the great Inca **Empire** long ago. The Inca were people who were united under one ruler. The Inca built cities and roads all across the Andes Mountains. They also had a huge and powerful army.

Who were the Inca? They left no written records. But people who study the ruins of Inca buildings and objects have learned some things. Stories from the past have also helped.

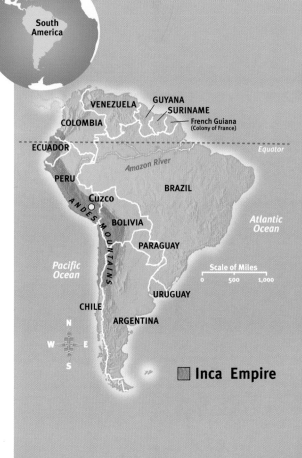

South America

VENEZUELA
GUYANA
SURINAME
COLOMBIA
French Guiana
(Colony of France)
ECUADOR
Equator
Amazon River
PERU
BRAZIL
Cuzco
Atlantic Ocean
BOLIVIA
PARAGUAY
Pacific Ocean
Scale of Miles
0   500   1,000
URUGUAY
CHILE
ARGENTINA
N
W   E
S
Inca Empire

We know that the Inca Empire came to an end in the 1500s when Spain **conquered** the Inca. But the Inca did not disappear. Some of the Inca ways of life are still followed today in South America.

The Inca people surrender to the Spanish.

In this book, you will read about the Inca Empire of long ago. You will learn about how the empire grew. And you will see what happened to end the Inca Empire.

THE RISE OF THE INCA EMPIRE

People have lived in South America since before history was written down. Humans moved south from North America many thousands of years ago. Some people settled in the Andes Mountains. The Inca were the last of many early peoples in South America.

▲ This was a village of people who lived before the Inca.

Learning About the Past

What we know about the Inca today comes from **archaeology** (ar-kee-AH-luh-jee). Archaeology is the study of the human past. Archaeologists dig in the places where ancient people lived. They look for the remains of buildings. They look for tools, weapons, and other objects made and used by people during their lifetime.

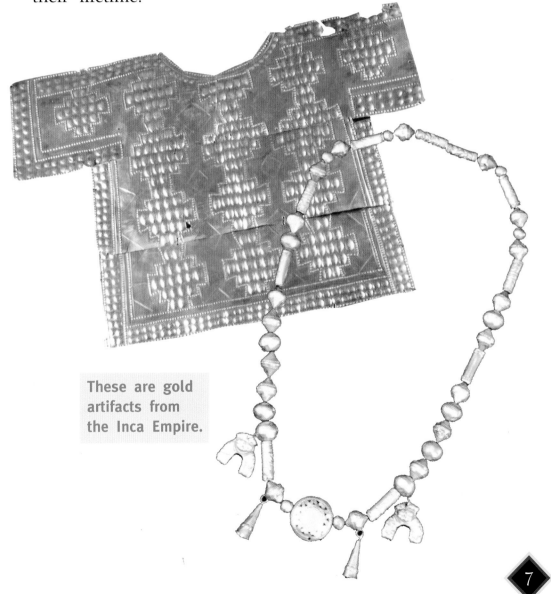

These are gold artifacts from the Inca Empire.

How the Inca Empire Came to Be

According to Inca legend, the Inca Empire began with eight people. This very old story says that the eight people were the ancestors of the Inca. This meant that they came before all the other Inca. One of the eight, Manco Capac (MAHN-koh KAY-pak), became the first Inca king. He and the other ancestors chose a place to begin a "Kingdom of the Sun." The place they chose was Cuzco.

At first, the Inca probably lived just in and around Cuzco. Then, they started to conquer other people who lived nearby. The Inca conquered more and more people until their empire grew very large.

POINT

Reread

Reread this page to find out how the Inca Empire grew. Share your findings with a classmate.

▲ Manco Capac

8

The Inca had twelve different kings. Not much is known about the first eight. The ninth king, Pachacuti (pah-chuh-KOO-tee), began conquering large parts of the Andes. He named himself "Sapa (SAH-puh) Inca," or supreme ruler. This meant that he had the highest power of anyone in the land.

Sapa Inca made many things happen under his rule. He forced conquered people off their land. He had his men build roads and raise crops on this new land. He spread the Inca religion.

▲ Pachacuti

1. SOLVE THIS

Who ruled longer, Sapa Inca or Topa Inca?

MATH ✓ POINT

What steps did you take to solve this problem?

The Last Four Inca Rulers

1400	1438	1471	1493	1527	1600
	Sapa Inca begins rule	Topa Inca begins rule	Huayna Capac begins rule	Atahualpa begins rule	

THE GREAT INCA EMPIRE

The Inca Empire reached its height in the early 1500s. The Inca called their empire "Land of the Four Quarters." The empire was divided into four quarters, or sections. Cuzco was at the center. The quarters stretched to the north, south, east, and west of Cuzco.

Cajamarca

Amazon River

Chancay Machu Picchu
Cuzco

INCA
EMPIRE

Lake Titicaca

ANDES MOUNTAINS

Pacific
Ocean

Atlantic
Ocean

N
W   E
S

Scale of Miles
0   500   1,000

Inca Empire

How the Empire was Organized

The Inca ruler controlled his empire. Each of the four quarters was divided into **provinces**. About 20,000 families lived in each province. A person loyal to the Inca king controlled each province. In this way, the king made sure that his subjects, or the people he ruled, were working for him.

A view of Lake Titicaca in Bolivia.
The Andes Mountains are in the background.

Cuzco

The city of Cuzco was the center of the Inca Empire. It was where the Inca **nobility** lived. The nobility were people like priests and royalty. Artists, weavers, and metalworkers came to Cuzco. Sons of conquered rulers were brought to Cuzco.

▲ Some buildings in Cuzco still have walls that were built by the Inca.

Cuzco was also the center of Inca religion. The Inca worshiped the sun. In Cuzco, they had a great temple dedicated to the sun god.

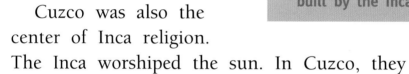

Keeping Records

To run his empire, the king had to remember important information. But the Inca had no writing. How could the Inca king keep this information?

The king had record keepers use special cords to keep records. The cords were bunches of knotted strings called quipus (KEE-pooz).

Record keepers used the knotted strings to record information about crops, herds of animals, and much more. Today, some experts believe the quipus may have been used to record stories.

▲ Each string in a quipu was used to record a different piece of information.

2. SOLVE THIS

The Inca tied knots in a string to record numbers. These strings were called quipus.

This quipu shows the number 132.

- hundreds
- tens
- ones

What number does this quipu show?

MATH ✔ POINT

How is the quipu like a place-value chart?

13

EVERYDAY LIFE OF THE INCA

In the Inca Empire, people had to do what the ruler and his officers said to do. The ruler even told people what they could and could not wear!

The sandals of Inca soldiers were made of leather and rope.

▲ wood carving of an Inca man

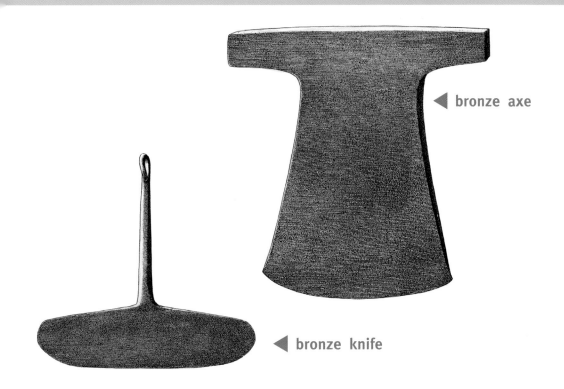

bronze axe

bronze knife

Life in the Empire

Most people in the Inca Empire lived in small villages. They spent their days farming. They had to give one-third of everything they grew to the ruler. The men also had to pay a labor tax to the ruler. The tax might be serving in the king's army. Or it might be helping to build a road or a building.

Many Inca subjects lived far from their native lands. Conquered people were often forced to move away from their home villages. They were sent to live in other parts of the empire.

POINT

Reread

How were Inca taxes different from the way taxes are paid today?

Growing Crops and Raising Animals

The Inca grew different kinds of crops, including corn, potatoes, squash, beans, and fruit. It was not always easy to grow food. Often, the Inca had to farm on steep hillsides. They cut flat areas into the hillsides to make fields to farm on. These flat areas looked like a staircase. Making these **terraces** was very hard work.

It's a Fact

The Inca grew more than 3,000 varieties, or types, of potatoes.

The Inca ate many different kinds of potatoes, even purple and pink ones!

This Inca terrace is still in use today.

Inca Messengers

The Inca needed a way to get news from one part of their large empire to another. They set up a system of runners to carry the news.

Every few miles along a road, a runner was waiting in a hut. The first runner would run to the second hut with the news. The second runner would run to the third hut with the news, and so on. Messages and goods sent through the runners could travel about 150 miles (240 kilometers) a day.

It's a Fact

The Inca kings in Cuzco used runners to bring them fresh fish from the Pacific Ocean. Cuzco was hundreds of miles from the Pacific Ocean. But the runners were so fast that the fish got to Cuzco without spoiling. And that's without ice!

◀ To save time, the new runner started running before the previous one stopped. Runners traded their messages and goods on the run.

Inca Storehouses

Men who worked on roads and buildings were away from home for a long time. So were men in the army. How did those men get the food and clothing they needed? The Inca set up storehouses in many parts of the empire. The storehouses held food, clothing, and other supplies for the men.

It's a Fact

After they conquered the Inca, the Spanish used the Inca storehouses. The food and other supplies they found in the storehouses lasted for twenty years!

3. SOLVE THIS

Imagine you are an Inca in charge of filling a storehouse. The army will arrive in your area in seven days. There will be 3,000 soldiers. Each soldier will need one pound of potatoes a day. Each soldier will also need three yards of cloth. The army will stay near your storehouse for three days. How many pounds of potatoes will you need? How many yards of cloth will you need?

MATH ✔ POINT

What information did you need to solve the problems? What information was not needed?

The Inca kept extra food and cloth in huge storehouses.

INCA ACHIEVEMENTS

The Inca are famous for their buildings made of stone. They built walls and buildings by fitting huge stones together. The stones fit together so well that even the blade of a knife could not slip between them.

4. SOLVE THIS

Most Inca could travel about 17 miles (27 kilometers) a day. If an Inca family traveled 68 miles (109 kilometers) on an Inca road, how many days would it take? How many rest stops would the family pass?

MATH ✔ POINT

What information from the text do you need to solve this problem?

Inca Roads

Inca roads were amazing. There were about 14,000 miles (23,000 kilometers) of roads. Two main roads ran north and south. One of the north-south roads went through the middle of the Andes Mountains. The other road was near the Pacific Ocean. Many small roads joined the two main roads. The Inca built rest stops along the roads. The rest stops were about one day's walk apart.

The Inca also built bridges across mountain streams and rivers. Travelers had to pay a toll to cross a bridge. Each bridge had its own toll collector who lived nearby.

▲ The Inca built bridges high in the Andes Mountains.

Machu Picchu

The Inca city of Machu Picchu (MAH-choo PEE-choo) was built more than 500 years ago. It is high in the Andes Mountains. Machu Picchu is completely invisible from the valleys below.

No one is really sure why Machu Picchu was built. Legend says that the city was built as a safe place for sacred Inca women. Most people believe that the city was built as a fortress for the Inca ruler.

They Made a Difference

An archaeologist named Hiram Bingham found Machu Picchu. The city was almost completely overgrown by jungle when he discovered it.

In about 1527, everyone suddenly left Machu Picchu. No one knows why this happened. For hundreds of years, no one lived in the city. No one seemed to know about it.

Then, in 1911, Machu Picchu was found again. The city was in **ruins**. But its beauty amazed those who saw it. People began to make special trips just to see the ruins. Machu Picchu has been visited by millions of tourists from around the world.

5. SOLVE THIS

Machu Picchu is about 50 miles (80 kilometers) from Cuzco. Cuzco is about 11,000 feet (3,400 meters) above sea level. Machu Picchu is about 8,000 feet (2,400 meters) above sea level. If you traveled from Cuzco to Machu Picchu, how much closer to sea level would you be?

MATH ✓ POINT

Write a number sentence you could use to find the answer.

THE SPANISH CONQUEST

In 1532, the Spanish conquered the Inca. More than 100 years of Inca rule came to an end. The Inca Empire was taken over by Spanish **conquistadors** (kahn-KEES-tuh-dorz). They were soldiers and explorers who came to South America looking for fame and riches.

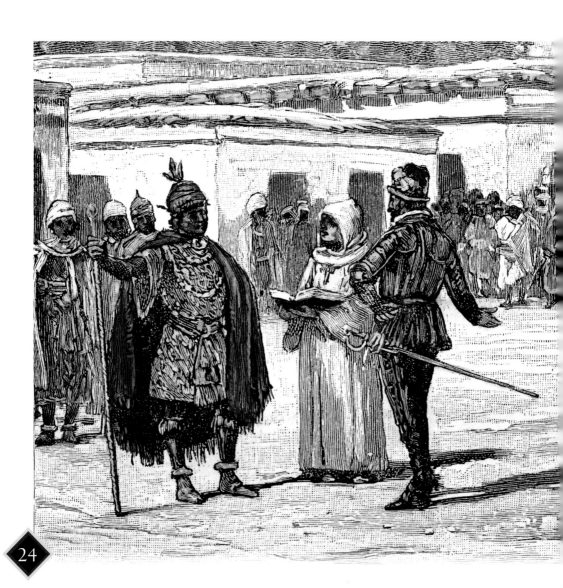

6. SOLVE THIS

How many years passed between Pizarro's two trips?

MATH ✓ POINT

What information from the text do you need to solve the problem?

Francisco Pizarro (puh-ZAR-oh) was a Spanish explorer.

Francisco Pizarro meets with Inca ruler Atahualpa.

He had heard tales about the riches in South America and wanted to travel there. Pizarro wanted to see for himself if he could find gold. In 1526, he and a group of men traveled along the coast of South America. But then, hungry and tired, Pizarro and his men turned around.

Pizarro did not give up. In 1532, he returned to South America. This time he brought 160 men. Pizarro and his men traveled into the Andes Mountains. They went to the town where the Inca ruler lived.

25

Capturing the Inca King

When Pizarro reached the town, it was empty. Everyone had gone to the countryside. That's where the Inca king and his army were. Pizarro guessed that the Inca king had about 80,000 soldiers. How could he and his band of 160 Spanish soldiers ever defeat them?

Pizarro had a plan. The town had a big central square. He ordered his men to hide in the houses around the square. Then he invited the Inca king for dinner. When the king arrived with some of his soldiers, Pizarro's men attacked. The Inca soldiers were defeated. The Inca king was captured.

End of the Inca Empire

The king was kept as a prisoner for many months. He was treated well, but he wanted to be free. He knew that the Spaniards wanted gold and silver. He told Pizarro that he would fill his prison room with gold and silver if Pizarro would free him.

Atahualpa
(ah-tuh-WAHL-puh)
was an Inca king.

▲ Atahualpa begged Pizarro to spare his life.

Pizarro agreed. Over the next several months, gold and silver objects were collected from all over the empire. The king filled his prison room as he promised. The Spaniards did not keep their promise, though. Once they got their riches, they killed the king.

7. SOLVE THIS

The floor of the room Atahualpa filled with gold was a rectangle. It measured 22 feet long and 17 feet wide. How many square feet is that?

MATH ✓ POINT

How do you know your answer is reasonable?

Once the king was killed, the Inca Empire began to fall apart. The conquistadors marched to Cuzco and claimed the empire for Spain. Spain would rule over the Inca for the next 300 years.

Spanish Colonial Rule

The Spanish brought diseases like measles with them. Millions of Inca died from the diseases.

For the Inca who lived, life was never the same. The Spanish divided the empire into huge farms. The Inca had to work on the farms for the Spanish.

> ## Historical Perspective
>
> **What might have happened to Pizarro and his men if the Inca had captured them? It is possible they would have been forced to farm for the Inca king, like all other Inca subjects.**

▲ By the middle of the 1500s, Spain had conquered large parts of South America.

CONCLUSION

Remains of the Inca Empire can be seen all over the Andes today. Inca buildings have lasted through many earthquakes and remain standing. Inca roads are still used in some places. What was the Inca empire like when it reached its biggest size? How did the Spanish take control of the Empire?

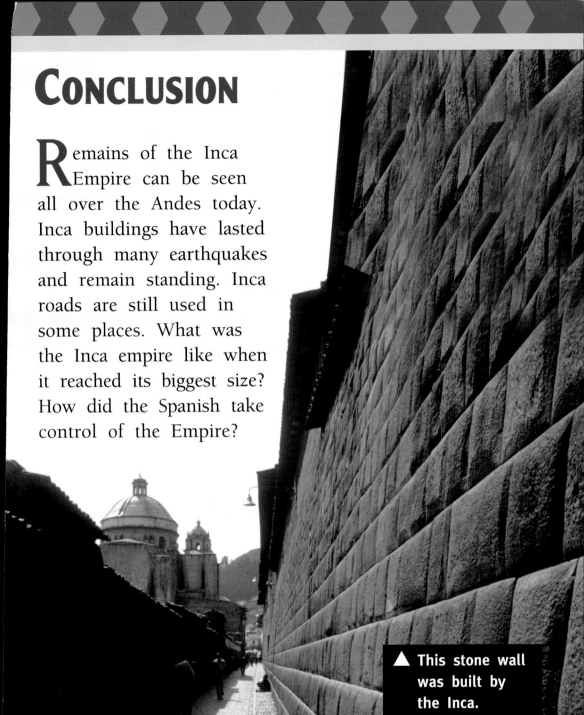

▲ This stone wall was built by the Inca.

The Last Four Inca Rulers

1400	1438	1471	1493	1527	1600
	Sapa Inca begins rule	Topa Inca begins rule	Huayna Capac begins rule	Atahualpa begins rule	

29

SOLVE THIS ANSWERS

1 **Page 9** Sapa Inca ruled longer. He ruled for 33 years. Topa Inca ruled for 22 years.

✔ **Math Check Point**
Step 1. Use information from the time line.
Step 2: Subtract to find out how many years each ruled. 1471 − 1438 = 33 and 1493 − 1471 = 22
Step 3: Compare the differences.

2 **Page 13** The number is 324.

✔ **Math Check Point**
The value of a number depends on its position in both the quipu and the place-value chart.

3 **Page 19** You would need 9,000 pounds of potatoes. 1 x 3 x 3,000 = 9,000. You would need 9,000 yards of cloth. 3 x 3,000 = 9,000

✔ **Math Check Point**
Information needed: the number of soldiers, the daily amount of potatoes for each, and the number of days they need food; the amount of cloth each soldier needs. Information not needed: the number of days before the army arrived.

4 **Page 20** It would take 4 days. Divide 68 miles by 17 miles a day. They would pass 3 rest houses on the way, since the rest stops were about one day apart.

✔ **Math Check Point**
The text tells you that the rest stops were about one day's walk apart.

5 **Page 23** You would be 3,000 feet closer to sea level.

✔ **Math Check Point**
11,000 − 8,000 = 3,000

6 **Page 25** Six years passed between the trips.
1532 − 1526 = 6

✔ **Math Check Point**
You need to find the dates of Pizarro's trips in the text.

7 **Page 27** The room is 374 square feet. 22 x 17 = 374

✔ **Math Check Point**
The answer 374 square feet is reasonable because it is close to the estimate of 400. 22 rounds to 20; 17 rounds to 20. 20 x 20 = 400.

GLOSSARY

archaeology   (ar-kee-AH-luh-jee) the study of the past through the things people have left behind (page 7)

conquered   (KAHN-kerd) taken over by force (page 4)

conquistador   (kahn-KEES-tuh-dor) Spaniard who conquered people for land and riches (page 24)

empire   (EM-pire) lands and people that are ruled by one person such as a king or emperor (page 3)

nobility   (noh-BIH-lih-tee) people of the upper classes (page 12)

province   (PRAH-vins) a region or area that is outside the capital city of an empire but under the control of the empire (page 11)

ruins   (ROO-inz) the remains of something destroyed, such as a building or object (page 23)

terrace   (TAIR-us) a flat step on a hill filled with earth that is used for planting crops (page 16)

INDEX